# Webbed words

(Selected Poems and Short Stories)

Millard Lowe

**Gotham Books**

30 N Gould St.
Ste. 20820, Sheridan, WY 82801
https://gothambooksinc.com/

Phone: 1 (307) 464-7800

© 2023 Millard Lowe. All rights reserved.

No part of this book may be reproduced, stored in a retrieval system, or transmitted by any means without the written permission of the author.

Published by Gotham Books (July 7, 2023)

ISBN: 979-8-88775-348-5 (sc)
ISBN: 979-8-88775-349-2 (e)

Because of the dynamic nature of the Internet, any web addresses or links contained in this book may have changed since publication and may no longer be valid.

The views expressed in this work are solely those of the author and do not necessarily reflect the views of the publisher, and the publisher hereby disclaims any responsibility for them.

# TABLE OF CONTENTS

Dedication ..................................................................................... 7
Foreword ....................................................................................... 8
Acknowledgements ..................................................................... 9
    For Karma Nurisha Wa Kupenda Lowe ............................. 10
    arising on a poetic morning… ............................................. 12
    free styling…because we're free… ..................................... 13
    in the surreal solemnity of nature ...................................... 15
    ponder this… ......................................................................... 16
    memories are forever… ........................................................ 17
    no vacancy… .......................................................................... 18
    through a pane's eyes… ........................................................ 19
    webbed .................................................................................. 20
    On A Mid-Summer Night .................................................. 21
    Night Light Variation in A Summer of Discontent ....... 22
    To A Super Lunar Score ..................................................... 23
    In The Realm of Circadian Times… .................................. 24
    Coiled Loneliness… .............................................................. 25
    From Rising To Setting ....................................................... 26
    Some Things Just Don't Last ............................................. 27
    Unwanted… ........................................................................... 28
    Water Trumpet ..................................................................... 29
    Abandoned Trunk… ............................................................. 30
    In The Autumn Of Her Life .............................................. 31
    Exodus Children and the Dream ....................................... 32
    To The Chosen Many ......................................................... 33
    I Am The River… ................................................................. 34
    Tuned Ebony Shades of Ecstasy ........................................ 35
    To Justice With Love ........................................................... 36
    Of Charcoal Memories ....................................................... 38
    To These Times .................................................................... 39

| | |
|---|---|
| At The Seashore with Watered Time | 40 |
| On Opportunistic Mesmerizing Media | 41 |
| Home to Misery | 42 |
| Standing On The Rock | 43 |
| The Bridge And The Fox | 44 |
| To Men Of Soul | 45 |
| A Sable Hued Syllabic Awakening | 46 |
| Haiku Moments | 47 |
| Haiku Rhythms | 48 |
| Haiku Melodies | 49 |
| Haiku Memories | 50 |
| Webbed Words | 51 |
| Part Two Short Stories | 55 |
| Life With Sami | 56 |
| Polecat | 63 |
| The Little Old Black Men Of The Quarters | 75 |
| A Pedagogical Odyssey | 83 |
| Prologue | 84 |
| Interlude | 91 |
| Epilogue | 95 |

# DEDICATION

To beloved sisters: Joyce, Norma and Sula. Stalwart Motherland Queens who continue to weave our extended family into a mosaic web of everlasting peace and love.

# FOREWORD

Like eagles, we soar; gliding through the sky of life. Though social turbulence challenges our rise, we continue to ascend—the horizon before us. Into the realm, like lions of Judah roaring, we leave woven trails and footprints of webbed words on the winds of time—flowing to the doorsteps of the reality of ourstory.

# ACKNOWLEDGEMENTS

Some of the short stories as well as some of the poems in this publication have been previously published by the author (including on several poetry websites). However, all copyrights© have been retained by the author.

# For Karma Nurisha Wa Kupenda Lowe

cosmic gem of the universe
exploded celestial beauty
princess of the milky way
poured into
the waiting womb
prepared

that's who you are

child of claimed prayer
moored on the shore of faith
anchored in the harbor of love

that's who you are

the north winked tonight
the crescent moon reclined—
what a glorious smile…reflecting

that's who you are

wait and be of good courage
the pain of joy is coming…wait…
pregnant belief has always delivered

that's who you are

yahweh has never failed
and never will—forever
you're ours and his blessed star

that's who you are

iv

some sarahs are of the heart
and not of the womb
the most high has much
mothering for you to do

that's who you are

twinkle…twinkle little star
blessed be the happiness
you bring

that's who you are.

n.b.: peace and love
that's who you are
dad.

# arising on a poetic morning...

as the sharp rays
of sunlight
meticulously sliced
through lingering clouds
to sculpt away
jagged edges
to scrape away
the corroded pain
of doubt,
today I will
pull out words
and paint
images of life
on a paper canvas—
chisel out a song of love
and feel and smell
the warm breath of god
soothing my sweet serene soul...

would if you would
arise
and journey with me
in the ecstasy
of a poetic odyssey—
wandering odin-like caverns
of the fertile womb
of my mind—
becoming one
with the morning's
dawning...

# free styling...because we're free...
## (improvisational notes reflecting ourstory)

sitting here
at the keyboard,
lettered blue notes
flow with rhythmic melodies
inking bars of varied clefts
of poetic pitch
rising from
b flat decrescendos
to c sharp crescendos
peaking trilling lights of truth
from a major second…

tuba blasting to depressed
notes now whining spine-tingling
wails john coltrane left behind
for you to forward
that we could go ahead
even when just sitting
parking
and monking around
in a blue note
frame of mind
undulating rivers
of memory bars
flowing to spirited shores
scattered with footprints
of giant steps
ancestors left
to the beginning

enabling us to ping whole notes
from the golden hieroglyphic
improvisations of ourstory
as we beat out polyrhythmic
emotions of the love supreme
that continues to keep and sustain us:

may the heat
of the ancestors' hearts
continue to radiate
and warm our melodic souls
with encore reverberations…

# in the surreal solemnity of nature

a solemn ant colony
passes in a funeral-like
procession
carrying bits of crumbs
and one of their own…

a lone ballooning spider
ceases his kiting
and hovers in mid-air…

hanging from its button
a chrysalis evicts
its metamorphosed tenant…

across the way
waddling mallards
halt oncoming traffic…

in a distant field
goats satisfy bulging cuds
with sweet chewed grasses…

one-by-one the solemn ants
descend a volcanic-like hole
of a huge temple-like mound…

as if descending a grave
the setting sun slowly sinks
below the horizon:
bidding a golden hued adieu….

## ponder this...

today we could blame the most high
for our condition
but to do so would be supercilious:
today is yesterday's child
and tomorrow's grandchild...

we cannot change yesterday
nor make today tomorrow
but we can do today
what we did not do yesterday...

come let us lay today
the foundation
for what must be completed
tomorrow:
ponder this...if you will....

## memories are forever...

the sun
announces the day
and night births
the moon
like cooling water
love quenches
the thirst of peace
and tranquility resides
in the mist of life
freedom must be
fought for and won
only life its self
is given
and in time
it too
is taken away
but memories…
memories
are forever…
memories:
cranial tombstones
of mental graves….

## no vacancy

pain
knocked at the door
last night…
love answered…invited it in…
fed it hope…
clothed it with faith
and showed it the back
exit…

# through a pane's eyes...

out in the summer's sun
on a bordering fence
a robin relaxed
while on the inner side
an unknown avian
strolled through the
bright green grass...

after pecking here and there
the unknown avian flew away—
no doubt the drum major
of the tailing parade
who likewise poised and peck
before taking flight...

a platoon of swallows landed
for a short survey and resumed flight—
a lone cardinal strutted by
and peered through the pane—
then gracefully flew away...

the fence's parallel pea green flora
swayed in the summer breeze:
a warm rhythmical moment
canvassed through opened blinds
of a panes eyes...

# webbed

mocking
innocence
a black widow
hung in her web
teasing passersby
so curious
their curiosity
became
a webbed experience

# On A Mid-Summer Night

Without belching
or hiccupping misty smoke,
the waiting sea
swallowed the setting sun;
the moon rose
and took her reflecting place
as the sky sprinkled its self
with twinkling stars.

Fire flies soared
to and fro nightshades
as if playing Marco Polo;
the whistling winds
taunting the fauna and floral.

In their usual stoic pose,
with big bulging eyes,
sager owls kept watch over
this shared canvassing of nature.

# Night Light Variation in A Summer of Discontent

The quite ebony night blew its warm teasing breath
taunting my wet shining sable skin with a faint coolness.
The paused crescent moon struggled with opaque-like clouds
to dispense sojourning light as it trekked across the sky
towards the self fulfillment of its circadian journey.

All around within the tree cribbed space,
fluttering little arthropods darted about—
flashing bits of light, as if to impart
pieces of truth the diabolical night offers
to those in the search there of: truth—
the light of the contemplating souls of darkness.

In the precinct of the darkness of night, light lurks—
always on patrol—juxtaposed superior twin:
blinking and winking behind guarded shades.

Thus, wherever darkness seeks to go and abide,
she finds companion light luring from the shadows:
welcoming her to coexist in peace, love and truth.

Soon, these cohabitating twins will usher in
another tomorrow. May God not forget and
so enlighten us—that we continue to strive to build
a new world order—reflecting peace, love and justice.

# To A Super Lunar Score

Cerulean mirror, true to color,
reflected the rouge hue
the setting sun left; a celestial beauty
that only the Supreme Architect could fashion.

That such cosmic beauty could have radiated
from a galactic scrapheap—once revered
an astral pearl—was beyond the limitations
of mere terrestrial comprehension.

Indeed, only the Sun of the Father could score
such a super sonata that only the planetary eyes
of Mother Earth could score.

# In The Realm of Circadian Times…

Oozed from my mother's womb
Like a butterfly wiggling from its cocoon
Separated free by nature—liberated together
Were we—and are we.

The sky has no limits—no borders—
Space's its extension—eternity its realm.
Down here in this land we are webbed around
Separated and bound one from the other
By the evil spun threads of human injustices.

History does not repeat—just changes methods;
Only nature is a true timed circadian rhythm in life.
History remains his story—methods altered as needed;

We are people of nature—survivors of the seasons and seasoning.
Ourstory must continue to be as the seasons—meeting each challenge
In the circadian rhythms of the time with likewise renewed strategies;
Like the sun of yesterday, we too must rise triumphantly to meet today.

# Coiled Loneliness

Beautiful little snake,
Coiled in her regal love—
So many warm hugs to share;
Fellow creatures pass and stare
But none has a stop to make…
Not even a cooing dove above.

Doomed to slither lonely in nature
Few if any, dare to pet and love her.
Warm affectionate hugs suspected,
She worms away alone and rejected;
Tell me…tell me please…for God's sake,
Why the fear of a poor little lonely snake?

# From Rising To Setting

She saw sunshine
shooting above
the horizon
exploding—
over pregnant
skies.

Sunset saw he son
shot in the back—
a black child stopped
on Morningside Drive:

In his hand
he held a ringing
cell phone

# Some Things Just Don't Last

Like a flash flood
you rushed into my life
plucking the strings
of my heart
with the fingertip ecstasy
of your ebon love.

Now I'm left
with climatic memories
and tears of mercy
washing away the agony.

The experience remains
a precious lesson
and climatic memories
remain priceless.

# Unwanted...

All alone
in the crowd…justice
standing…seeking someone
to please.

Like a lonely fish
swimming in a school,
she bites a baited hook.

Reeled in…she's scaled
and thrown back—
unwanted.

# Water Trumpet

Under quiet
sunshine
lonely conch shell
sits…
Tides
ebb and flow—
ancestor's echoes
leap
into my ear…

# Abandoned Trunk...

There lay an old gray trunk;
Never to hold any thing again.
There in the wet soil,
A wrinkled decaying lump.
Stilled in the soft gentle rain;
Lifeless: without coil.

Gone are the traveling memories
And self gushing showers;
Leaving only companion ivory
To be tombstone flowers.

Thus is the sad fate
Of a great regal elephant;
Victim of greed's sake—
And man's pleasured hunt.

# In The Autumn Of Her Life

Beneath the cold gray skies, proudly she stood.
Stripped bare, naked to the world; arms outstretched.
Unashamed and poised in anchored dignity, she stood:
Unabashed, she stood.

Through the peep-holes of window shades,
Eyes have reached out—touching her beauty:
This ancient lady—
An old tree glorified in the autumn of her life.

Now I stand atop this scenic autumn hill, glorifying
My ebony Mother—victimized, stripped bare of God given rights.
Yet, with arms outstretched and poised in her anchored dignity,
This ebony queen mastered each day in the autumn of her life: Yes,
Unabashed, she stood.

# Exodus Children and the Dream

Though time tested and weary worn,
We remain steadfast in the perilous journey.
You cannot beat us down with you scorn;
Nor destroy us with hate and abject illegality.
In the hour of darkness and the gloom of day,
The struggle will continue and shall never cease.
Liberation is a process allowing nothing to get in its way;
The table has turned; the shorn no longer fears the beast.
The story has already been told; we're children of the Exodus;
Across the deserts and over the sea floors our souls have gone.
There is nothing in your narrow-mindedness that can stop us;
No shootings or bombings can prevent the dream reaching home.
Many beautiful lives we have lost; but not our sacred hope;
And what once was despair, is now just a simple footnote.

# To The Chosen Many

To those who are black,
We've come too far to turn back;
To those who are white, stand up and fight
For what's truly right;
To those of another color—colors
**Remember, we're all sisters & brothers;**
For those who feel left out,
Here's what it's all about:
Irrespective of race or gender,
To the bigoted demons, let us **never surrender**.

# I Am The River...

I am the river.
I'm poured out
of God's
celestial cistern:
a full river
swollen with His tears.

I am the river.
My banks hold
the flow
of a nation:
denied, crucified, died,
resurrected and sanctified.

I am the river.
My tributaries flow
wide and deep—

outward, inward, upward,
downward, and back
to the source.

I am the river.
I'm the flowing essence
of a mother's womb—
Come
wade in my history—
let the wetness of ourstory
bathe away all your delusions.

# Tuned Ebony Shades of Ecstasy

Here we are,
black as the night;
sable souls singing songs
of Nubian love—Slow dancing
on opaque rhythmic nimbus clouds;

Unshackled melodies of generations
flowing from charcoal tributaries
slowly undulating—Streaming
between ebony sheen banks;

Estuaries of ecstasy splash joyously
into the wetness
of the dark hued sea of our love;
Tuned and harmonized
in the abyss of relief,
fading moans moor themselves:
waiting the coming of the next tide.

# To Justice With Love

Your deceitful tease
and illusiveness
are beyond compare;
your blind promise
has yet proven
fool I was, thinking
such also included me.

I'm taught
to always love
and seek you
everywhere;
but in all my loving
and searching,
I can't find you
anywhere.

For me, the warmth
of your sweet bosom
has never been there.
Yet, I shall not wander in vain
nor without a strong belief—that
from your aching judicial loins—
unfailing faith will bring sweet relief.
that you really care.

How long
must my soul
lowly hang
like strange fruit
dripping trails

of its fallen red juice
behind its every pursuit?

They say
only death rivals
your equanimity;

# Of Charcoal Memories

Black as the night
My sable soul sings songs
Of Nubian ancestors
Sleeping behind closed eyes
In the depths of the inner sanctum
Of the womb of mind—silhouettes
Of beings peeking through dark skies
Across ebony horizons;

Granny said, "The blacker the berry,
The sweeter the juice", that "I was
Created in the image…"
That "God don't ugly…made none
But the crème de la crème…"
That, "like the ivory clouds of the sapphire sky",
I too, am the apple of His eye.

# To These Times

Today
time took time
to think

Then truth
took thinking time
to task:

Testing teasing themes
that today taught—
trouncing telltale tragedies.

# At The Seashore with Watered Time

Laying there at the shore,
My aloe ebony sheen body
Basking beneath palm shaded skies,
The naked winds deposited their coolness
Blending their echoes with the flowing tides';

Struggling for contentment in solitude,
I looked out over waves whose watered ancestors
Spilled onto these same shores with ancestors of mine;

In this agonizing beauty of cerulean sea
And salt hued sands, whispering ghost voices
Of those who sounds drowned at sea,
Shattered settled silence streaming stolen space.

Gazing into the distance—east of the shore,
My eyes—through swelling tears—captured
A dark hued turtle emerging from mortal remains
Of a fallen decaying coconut tree—his eyes stayed on the sea.
Slowly, but with determined effort, he scurried onward
Towards the ebbing tides with his free flapping feet;
Disappeared over the waiting horizon—liberated.

Refueled and energized with like determination and will,
I again clothed myself with undaunted courage and faith.
Belted with the hope the sea has in its waters, I anchored my soul;
Returned to the struggle; assured that never has it been in vain.

Indeed, a pause at the sea shore can be invigorating to the struggling spirit;
*For has it not been written*: The workers of iniquity…shall soon be cut down…?
Yes…and we the captured chosen children of God shall rise…as did the blessed Rose.

# On Opportunistic Mesmerizing Media

They say that opportunity is everywhere; so are we.
For who does the bell tolls? Certainly not for you and me;
Except to rid us of the rolls;

From the body to the mind, they're still trying
To shackle ancestral heirs of those
Their ancestors stole;
Still trying with deceit and abject political lying:
Failing to see that we are the heirs
Of the brave and the bold;

Indeed, opportunity is found everywhere
And the opportunists are taking full advantage.
Let us not be caught off guard but be totally aware;
24-7 mass media, we must carefully manage.

Yes, tech media has become the new control
Of you and me;
24-7, we are hooked on their planned media fix
Of mesmerizing apathy;

How soon we have forgotten the opportunistic exploitations
In our beloved country's by-polar racial and gender relations;
Once again we are being hoodwinked by deceptive bigotry
To keep the focus away from what's happening to you and me.

# Home to Misery...

Deceit wears a Janus face;
its self veiled in angelic façade
whose fixed smile
is magnetized mesmerism;

Unhappiness breeds contempt
teasing innocence
into its woven web of misery;

Morality, not favored nor desired,
decayed in the cocooned cell
created in the web's confining labyrinth;

Compassion, a stranger of instinct,
has failed to be learned—Suffering relieved
only by that of others—What greater healing
than injecting such on those once loved?

Bereft of reasoning, misery seeks misery
and forgiveness remains an elusive discovery;
tears, an unemotional exhaust of afterthought;
leaving a dry mirroring sheen—Cracked.
Cracked and washed away with morning shower.

How long before the reservoir of grief
runs dry;
and the cistern of love overflows?

# Standing On The Rock

The bones of ancestors are rattling …shaking—
Itching from infectious dust of stagnation;
Aware we must be …Liberty is not a rock
And we're not children of Sisyphus—nor
Weak branches fallen from the ancestral vine.
We are the children of Light—of the Lamb
And the Lion—soaring on the wings of the Bird
Of all creatures—to whom roadblock rocks
Are like the shells of historical eggs—here …before us.
As we ascend the preverbal rock of freedom's mountain,
Let us not tread in darkness nor rest in stagnation.
Let our pausing be mere moments of reflection—Meditating.
Finding new strategies to meet and conquer new challenges.

Come…let us travel the sojourn of our ancestors—plunging deep
Into our story—rising in the spiraling smoke of memory—revealing
Traveled paths of once alien mountains lined with whispering trees
Marking …Lighting the way of the prophetic underground journey.
Justice today …like roaches and time…remains elusive—a ghosting;
But—like truth—though crucified …will not be denied its Easter.
Indeed—Out of the ashes of lies—the Phoenix of Liberation rises…
Leaving behind nightmares of setbacks, releasing prophetic visions
Giving reality to promised freedom at last—standing on the Rock of Life.

PostScript: "And they that wait upon the Lord shall renew their strength; they
Shall mount up with wings as eagles; they shall run, and not be weary;
And they shall walk and not faint."

# The Bridge And The Fox

Quietly spanning the space
over the banks separating two sides
by a river whose waters
are tinted ruby red
with blood—you stand.
Only the fox dare
challenge your expanse
with its adept incendiary
cunningness—sneaking
back and forth
with precious booty
filling allied shelves—
pleasuring den mates.
Though paw-prints dot
the slippery surface…
no trails are on either side—
only the collateral chaos
that sly cold war maneuvers
leave behind:
meanwhile—a confused world
sits by…palming its head…pondering
the latent weirdness of it all.

# To Men Of Soul

That Achebe should herald us *men of soul*—
repositories of the spirits of the ancestors—
Ancestors rooted deep
in the earth of our hearts.
The sovereignty
they have chosen to bequeath
to those sons landed here
must not be bastardized with retreat—
dissolution…secret evasion—ethnocide.
We are the longevity vases
of the stems of our beginnings;
soul water holes for the revitalization
of the spirits of faith.
Far be from it…that despair—
that grim tenant…be allowed
to find lodging in the loop-holes
and setbacks of the struggle.
Indeed, let not the weight
of deferred dreams…shadowed
visions and broken promises
crush the pillars of hope
that uphold the temples of our faith.
Let us not forget—men of soul—ours
is the mission possible…to smash divisiveness…
disconnectedness…and suspect—
bringing healing and wholeness of unity
in our struggle for total liberation.
Come brethren—men of soul…with God…
with the breastplate of His liberating love…come
let us strengthen ourselves for the journey—
leaving ancestral footprints for our children to plod.

# A Sable Hued Syllabic Awakening...
## (For Richard Wright)

Even snakes have love...
but no one wants their embrace;
such coiled loneliness...

Yet nature provides...
eggs are laid...babies are hatched
and snakes slitter on.

Pity...we're not snakes...
our eggs denied their seeds...
food for the human mongoose.

Yet...we are like dough...
rising in our due season...
and nature provides the time.

Hunger games return...
and the predators are back;
let the prey prepare...

Let the fire this time
be a control burn...clearing
our path to justice...

Freedom is not free...
it must be fought for and won:
Johnson...Ali...Us....

# Haiku Moments...

Evaporating...
Daily giving up water...
The sea...always full...

Fires burning down trees...
We send prayers up for rainfall,
Mud pulls down our homes...

Looking for the sun,
A worm came out of his hole...
A bird greeted him.

The pond...home sweet home;
    The frog lays her eggs there:
        Fish stop by to eat.

        Beautiful peacock...
Flouting her rainbow feathers....
    Pity...she can't fly...

# Haiku Rhythms

The winter wind blows
The willow tree waves its leaves
Watching clouds turn dark

Trees shedding their leaves
Old winter taking her toll
Spring will bring revenge

Twinkling little stars…
Quiet…rhythmic music plays…
Eyes see…the mind hears…

Nature's symphony
A nocturnal overture
Darkness…frogs…crickets

Sunshine—leaves blowing…
Tree shadows wave on the ground,
What will the moon bring?

# Haiku Melodies

Chrysalis hanging…
Monarchs emerging…soaring…
Spring…summer…coming

Fireflies blinking lights
Stars streaking across the sky
Shinning moon watching

Trees have leaves again
Ariel tenants return
Spring's in charge again

Quiet lake…floating ducks
Baited fishing lines plopping…
Silent sun setting…

Praying mantis kneels…
Such pious genuflection…
Naïve prey stunned

# Haiku Memories

Under dark blue skies
Happy children played hopscotch
Thunder cracked...bombs fell

The night skies lit up
Thunderous sounds filled the air
It was not a storm

A single dark fruit...
Hanging...rotting in moonlight...
A strange fruit indeed...

The skies were crying
Pecking birds flew to their nest
Worms had a party

Life and dying...
Juxtaposed realities:
The cradle and grave...

# Webbed Words...

Spun webbed words weave true tales
knitted and woven with worn threads
spooled from the loom of keloid memories:
experienced sojourns on the cross of time.

                        Webbed words spun.

So many suns have risen and gone down;
so many moons have waxed and waned;
so many tears and much blood have fallen.

                        Webbed words spun.

We've sailed many seas; crossed many rivers;
climbed many mountains; trekked many valleys;
we've downed many Jericho walls. Yet
many more challenges remain to be conquered.

                        Webbed words spun.

While we may no more be where we once were, yet
we're not near to where we ought to be.
The destiny of our total liberation remains to be manifested.

                        Webbed words spun.

The web of our reality catches fertile tomorrows
pregnant with new sons and new daughters—
cocooned warriors evolving to sting and plague
injustice and deceit; warriors soaring with liberation's
quivered arrows inked with written webbed words—
Weapons in the struggle: free your mind and you are.

                        Webbed words spun.

No longer can the black holes of ignorance,
apathy and deceit, deter us! No longer
can black holes of bigotry and racism stop us!
Black holes of injustice and genocide delete us!

                              Webbed words spun.

There's no stopping us now! We are free! Free!
The promise land is freedom of mind. Get ready y'all!
A train's coming…whistle blowing…bells ringing…!

                              Webbed words spun.

# PART TWO
## SHORT STORIES

# LIFE WITH SAMI

As if she had an innate alarm clock within her brain, around 6:30 AM each day, Sami began her morning ritual. It began with irritating whining howls. She would then stretch in a way that formed her back into a lying down crescent-like shape that caused her spine to crack. She would next shake off whatever had become a part of her fur while she slept. Then she would yawn in a slow, wide mouth fashion that reminded you of a snake disjointing its jaw to swallow captured prey. It was weird…really weird!

We had adopted Sami through a rescue program. What a pitiful sight she was. She was a mistreated abandoned pup. A Shih Tzu! Although she had been shampooed and well fed, her frail body and sad eyes made it seem as if she had walked all the way from China! After 6 months, numerous trips to the Vet, and hundreds of hours of tender paternal care, she had become the cutest little ugly dog you ever wanted to see. The fur of her trunk, tail and upper legs was pearly white. Her lower legs and head had a beautiful golden-beige color. Her ears were mostly white with the lower part having that golden-beige color. And when you would look in her eyes, she would just melt you away. She was indeed, a pooch extraordinaire. For a dog, she had so many human qualities. As any child or grand-child would, there were days that she put our tolerance to the ultimate test. We always tried to get to sleep before Sami did. For once that little doggie went to sleep she went into an asthma-like kind of snoring that put even my Auntie Ida Mae's snoring to shame. And this lasted most of the night. Sometimes, I felt like we should have named her Ida Mae instead of Sami.

Down through the past three generations of my extended family, Auntie Ida Mae had become infamous for her unique snoring manner. I remember that when I was a kid, we thought that she must have been the world champion snorer of all times. You could hear her snorts and grunts all over the place. Even when loud music was playing or the TV volume was high. Her husband, Uncle Doughbelly, use to say that she was calling hogs. Every hog within ten miles must have heard her!

I remember one night when Auntie Ida Mae's snoring got so bad it scared us nearly to death! My sisters and I were downstairs watching the TV when we suddenly heard these strange sounds coming from Auntie Ida Mae's bedroom. We ran upstairs to her bedroom and nearly broke the door down! She never missed a beat in her snoring! The sound was frightening! Baby Sister suggested we do something quick before she choked to death. I clapped my hands really loud and screamed boo! Auntie Ida Mae grunted, quietly turned over and let go of one that sounded like a 57 Chevrolet with a gutted muffler! Baby Sister shouted out, "Jesus Christ! Is she dead?" No sooner than the words jumped out of Baby Sister's mouth, Auntie Ida Mae resumed her hog calling. It seemed like she was having some weird dream that increased and amplified her snoring. We giggled and ran downstairs to the kitchen. Uncle Doughbelly, with his big stomach hanging over his belt, was sitting at the kitchen table sipping on a hot toddy. It was his nightly ritual. One in which he hoped would enable him to go upstairs and get to sleep before the hog calling got loud. Like Aunt Ida Mae, Sami must have also had some weird dreams. Sometimes, her snoring was often interrupted with rhythmic, muffled barks. I remember reading some time ago that dogs, like humans, also dream. Sometimes Sami acted more human than dog.

Each morning after her stretching routine, Sami would go through the doggie door onto the veranda to do her business. For this purpose, we had purchased a little artificial green golf putting mat from K-Mart. I laugh every time I think about the day we bought that little green mat.

"How are you two lovely people doing this fine morning?" the cashier said.

"Just fine; thank you," Queen replied

"Can I help you folks find anything else?"

"No. Thank you. We're good," I replied.

The little cashier kept chatting away as she checked and bagged our things. She tied a string around the rolled up green mat and handed it to me.

"I hope this is going to help you improve your golf game."

"I think my golf game is about as good as it is going to get," I said.

"Y'all have a nice day, now. And don't forget to come back to see us."

When we got to the car, Queen asked, "What did you mean about your golf game is about as good as it's going to get. Man, you've never even picked up a golf club." I laughed and replied, "And I don't intend to either. What did you expect me to say? I was not about to tell her that this was going to be used as a dog's poop lawn."

"Man, you crazy," Queen said.

"I'll tell you what's crazy," I replied.

"What?" Queen responded.

"What's crazy is paying somebody one million dollars to spend a whole day walking over yards of pretty green grass just to knock a little bitty white ball into a little black hole. Do you know how many houses could be built for the homeless on the golf courses in this country?" I sarcastically said.

"You do have a point there, but…" Before Queen could finish, I interrupted.

"Now, don't get me wrong. I am not mad at Tiger. He's…" Before I could finish, Queen interrupted me.

"You ready?"

"Yes. Everything is in the car. Let's go."

Early in the morning, after having gone out and taken care of her doggie business, Sami returned to the bedroom and began tugging at the bed coverings. I glanced over and noticed that it was now 6:45 AM. I then glanced over at Queen and noticed that she was still sleeping. Undoubtedly, she must have been dreaming. There was a cute little smile across her face. At any rate, I threw off the covers, got up and went into the bathroom. I relieved myself, brushed my teeth, and washed my face. When I was done, I put on my robe and went into the kitchen and began preparing breakfast for the three of us.

Sami took her usual spot at the entrance to the kitchen where she could observe my every movement. She sat there panting away. Her drooling tongue hung out of the left side of her mouth. The expression on her little doggy face seemed to be saying, "You ain't got my breakfast ready yet?" Usually, I had to prepare her breakfast first.

Aroused by the aroma of breakfast, Queen got up and came into the kitchen and made her regular cup of coffee. Coffee was the one thing I didn't drink. So, making coffee was one thing she didn't expect me to do. The last time I had made coffee, Queen complained that it tasted like mud. I remember saying, "What's wrong? When I was a kid, mud cakes tasted pretty good to me." Queen looked over at me and said, "Fool, when you were a kid, gas was 28 cents a gallon. And for a quarter, you could buy a movie ticket, a bag of popcorn, and a soda. And you could go down to the store and buy cigarettes one at a time." I smiled and kept doing what I was doing. I was pleased that I didn't have to make coffee.

After breakfast, Queen and I sat down to catch up on the world news. I changed the TV channel from OWN to CNN, to see what was happening around world. Ebola was becoming a pandemic and seemed to have been the only true democratic thing happening around the world. It furthered appeared that it had now become as easy to sneak into the White House as it was to sneak into a movie. And it looked like wars were being fought on almost every continent. What was this world coming too? After a few minutes of such depressing news, I switch the channel to the Steve Harvey Show.

That evening while we were getting ready for bed, Queen for some reason felt it necessary to remind me of my upcoming prostate exam and colonoscopy. Why she needed to remind me, I don't know. No man in his right mind would forget those two appointments.

"Why did you have to remind me? You know how I hate those exams. Damn!"

"That's why I'm reminding you! There are just too many Black men dropping dead from double C."

"Double C…what's that?" I asked.

"You know…prostate cancer and colon cancer."

Catching the seriousness in Queen's voice, my thoughts flowed back to my Uncle Doughbelly. Before he died, he had told us that the reason he kept getting up throughout the night to go to the bathroom, was because of Auntie Ida Mae's hog calling snoring, and the hot toddy he drank before going to bed. Later on, we found out that that was not the real reason he kept getting up so much. Not being one who regularly went to the doctor, it was too late when we finally found out that he had prostate cancer. He died a year after the diagnosis.

Regaining my composure, I said, "You know Queen, the colonoscopy itself, is not so bad. It's the preparation the night before that I dread. That cocktail they give you does a real job on you." Continuing, I said, "At least that castor oil and orange juice wash-out the old folks gave us every summer allowed you a couple of days. But the stuff the doctors give you these days does a Niagara Falls on you overnight! And I mean all night!" I was being funny, but also serious. Queen laugh so hard the whole bed shook. Then she said, "If I would have had that cocktail an hour before, I would not be able to laugh like this." I laughed. "Yeah, I know what you mean", I said. "Remember that time I sneezed after having drunk that stuff an hour before?" Queen replied, "Do, I? Whew!" We both started laughing.

We laughed until tears rolled down our cheeks. We somehow always found something funny about the most serious things. It was a coping method we had perfected to keep us from going crazy with the things we had to deal with to survive the daily trials and tribulations of life. And believe me, like everyone else, we had our fair share of trials and tribulations.

Aroused by the loud laughter, Sami came trotting into the bedroom. She stopped at the foot of the bed. Sitting down on her haunches and wagging her tail, she looked up at us laughing. The expression on Sami's face was like that of a person who had just seen two other people who had obviously just lost their minds. We stopped laughing.

"Did you take your meds?" Queen asked.

"Yes," I replied. "Did you take yours?"

"Of course, I did. Turn off the lights and turn down the TV."

"Yeah", I said. "Let's try to get to sleep before Sami starts her nightly sleeping spasms."

The next morning was weird. I mean really weird. Sunlight had begun to creep through the partially opened blinds. The TV timer had turned off the television. The bedroom was dead quiet. I blinked my eyes and looked over at the clock. To my surprise, it was already 7:30 AM! I got up. Still blinking my eyes to get used to the daylight, I made my way to the bathroom. When I came out, I became aware that I had completely overlooked Sami lying there at the foot of the bed.

"Queen...Queen! Wake up!"

"What...what is it?"

"It's Sami! She is not making any noise!"

"What!" Queen sat up in the bed. She leaned over the foot of the bed and looked down at Sami's lifeless body on the floor. She cupped her hands over her mouth and her eyes began to tear up. "Oh no, no, no...my poor little baby." I walked over to the window and opened the blinds wider. A cloud had drawn a curtain over the sun and the sky was beginning to sprinkle rain. I walked back over to the bed and put my arms around Queen. I gently kissed each of her watery eyes. I could almost taste the grief in her salty tears. I could feel the trembling grief of her body.

"It's starting to rain, Queen," I said, "You know back in Jamaica, they say that when a person dies and it rains, it is a sign of the goodness of that person." Queen just sat there with her nose running and tears rolling down her cheeks.

"Damn that! Queen said as the tears continue to flow, "this ain't Jamaica! She was such a good little girl, Leon. She was my baby..."

"I know my love, I know."

"You're my baby too, honey. Lord, give me strength," she said.

We got up and went outside to the storage shed and took out a small purple box. Kissing Queen on her salty cheek, I said, "She should fit in here." A soft smile spread across Queen's face.

"You know, we never got her those cute little doggie slippers," she said.

"Well she won't need them now", I replied. "She's gone on to dog heaven now."

"I know, Leon", Queen replied with a smile, "her little feet will be up there trotting on soft cotton clouds."

Both of our eyes were now filled with tears. Wiping away each other's tears, we both smiled and began to laugh.

"She gave us so much joy. Didn't she?" I said.

"She sure did," Queen replied.

We spent most of that night laughing and talking about all the years of fun we had with Sami in our lives. We agreed that although we would miss Sami dearly, we would not try to replace her. After all, Sami was not just a pet. She was a member of the family. 14 years is a long time in dog years.

It was well after midnight before we eventually gave in to sleep. Queen dozed off first. After I heard what I thought was a slight snore, I turned off the TV and gave a shout out, "Alexia, play John Coltrane…A Love Supreme". I have no idea what time I fell asleep.

# POLECAT

Towards the end of 2007, Sean Smith and Heather Malveaux were probably the two happiest people in the world. Sean had just received his officer's commission in the military and Heather, his fiancée, had recently completed her RN Master's degree. In three months they were to be married. The date had been set for January 2. They had already taken out a one year lease on a two bedroom detached condominium home where they planned to have their small wedding in the fenced backyard.

The community in which Sean and Heather had moved into was close to both the military base and the city's general hospital. This was convenient for both of them insofar as driving back and forth to work was concerned. It was particularly good for Heather. Being a Head Nurse, she periodically had to work a 12-hour shift. On such occasions, a short drive home was indeed a blessing in disguise. Things were coming together very well for them. But things were soon to change.

On one of Heather's days off, she decided that she would make gumbo for dinner. This was one of Sean's favorite dishes. He loved seafood and okra gumbo. Particularly, over a big bowl of Uncle Ben's rice. On the side, he would usually have potato salad, French-style bread, and a cold beer. While preparing the gumbo, Heather amused herself listening to a CD of a Pattie Labelle concert. When she had finished preparing dinner, she sat down to catch up on her TV recordings of *Scandal*, while she waited for Sean to come home.

When Sean pulled into the driveway, he did not open the garage door immediately. Rather, he sat in the car in deep thought for about five minutes. When he finally went inside, Heather was absorbed in her show. The aroma of gumbo saturated the whole house. Sean leaned over and gave Heather a kiss on the top of her head.

"Hi, Baby. Damn! It smells good in here."

"Hey, Boo. How was the day?"

"Oh, you know, just another day at the office."

Sean went over to the bar and poured out a Hennessey. He took a sip of his drink and went over and sat down next to Heather.

"After dinner, we need to talk Baby."

"Ok", Heather said. "You sure you don't want to talk about whatever it is now?"

"After dinner Baby, right now that gumbo is calling my name! But finish watching your

TV show. Then we can eat."

Heather continued to watch the end of her recorded shows. But she found it difficult to concentrate on what the characters were saying to each other. Her mind was on what Sean had said. They needed to talk. She knew from experience, that whenever Sean used that expression, something serious was going on. Sean sat down next to Heather, and with his head on her shoulder, watched the end of the TV recordings with her. Now she knew something was wrong. Sean had never been too fond of this TV show.

Apart from loudly blessing the food, Sean and Heather enjoyed dinner in silence. While this may have been a discomfort for some people, experience had taught Heather that when Sean ate in silence, it was a sign that the food was really good. Yet, she still wondered what Sean wanted to talk about. She decided to initiate conversation.

"Hon, what is it that we need to discuss?"

"Oh, I got some bad news today, Baby," Sean replied, as he got up and went to the bar to get another drink.

"What's going on, Hon?"

"Well...I was informed that my Unit was being deployed."

"What...you got'a be kidding me!" The tone of Heather's voice and the expression on her face mirrored her surprise and disgust.

"When," she asked. Tears leaked from her eyes and slowly flowed down her cheeks.

"That's just it Baby...they...they're talking about two weeks from now," Sean answered. The frustrations he felt were obvious by the sound of his voice and the quivering of his lips.

"No, this cannot be happening. Don't they know that we have a wedding in about six weeks? It's not fair! Damn it!" Heather said as she stood up, waving her hands in the air. She ran her tongue across her top lip, tasting the salty tears that had now reached her mouth. "It's not fair…" Her sobs had now drenched her face.

"I know, Baby," Sean said, as he walked over and embraced Heather, gently kissing her salty lips. "As far as the military is concerned, it's duty and honor first. Everything else comes second…even family. But we'll work it out, Baby. We'll work it out. Every little thing is going to be alright. We'll just have to inform everyone that the wedding has been set back until I return." Sean's words seemed to simply float in the air. He again kissed Heather's salty lips. The reservoir of his own tears began to leak as he gently held her, struggling to console both himself and Heather.

That was the day that the plans Sean and Heather had made to spend the rest of their lives together began to fall apart. The wedding was postponed until after Sean's return. Arrangements were made to have three-fourths of his pay to be sent to Heather so that she could maintain the household and set up a second savings account. This account would enable them to amass a little cushion during Sean's 6 months of deployment.

During Sean's first two months of deployment, Heather wrote to Sean once a week. His replies usually took several weeks. Sean had now been gone almost four months and Heather had only heard from him three times. One day around the end of the fourth month, when Heather opened the mailbox and saw a letter from Sean, her heart skipped a beat. *Thank God. He's alive. And he'll soon be home*, she said to herself. Back in the house, her hands were shaking so much that she had to pause and take a deep breath to collect herself before opening Sean's letter.

As Heather read the passionate words of the first two pages of the letter, she was all giggles, and there was a gingerly tingling in her thighs. But as she began to read the third page, the words became less passionate. Then she came to those devastating words, *so we've been informed that because of the intensity of the campaign, our deployment has been extended another three months*. Heather fell to her knees and began sobbing. "No!" she screamed. I can't take this…I can't take it! She stretched out on the floor and cried herself to sleep.

Another five months passed before Sean returned home from his tour of duty. However, he had become a changed man. Whenever Heather mentioned wedding plans, Sean would reply, "Give me some time to adjust, Baby." Heather also noticed that he had begun to drink more than usual. When he came home from the military base, the first thing he would do was to pour a drink before saying anything to her. When Heather would ask how things were going at the Base, Sean would simply say, another day at the office. But what troubled Heather most, was the change in their sex life. The once gentle Sean had become more animal-like in what use to be, lovemaking. Now, it was as if he was struggling to relieve himself of the frustrations of an animal being in heat!

Those long months in the Middle East had done a real head job on Sean. However, the straw that broke the camel's back, insofar as Heather was concerned, was when Sean came home and told her he had volunteered for another tour of duty.

"Have you gone out of your cotton picking mind," replied Heather, amplifying her contempt and hurt.

"That's just it, Baby. I need to do this in order to get my head together," Sean had answered. "Besides, it will bring in more money, enabling us not only to go on and get married but also enable us to put a down payment on a mortgage for a larger place."

"But what about me Sean; did it not occur to you to discuss all of this with me before going off and volunteering to fight for somebody else's freedom while we're still catching hell right here at home.? Jesus Sean! This crap has gone too far!"

Her pain was further magnified as she recalled how happy she had been earlier in the day when the doctor had told her that she was pregnant! She was so hurt and angry that she kept the news to herself.

During his first two months of his second deployment, the letters between Heather and Sean were infrequent; and their content was more like that between pen pals. By the third month, there was no communication between them at all. She had never mentioned to Sean that she was pregnant. Then one day around the middle of the fifth month after Sean had been gone, Heather received a communication informing her that Sean had been declared MIS or had become a POW. Heather was devastated. Her whole world had become shattered. All she could do was pray, hope, and wait.

After 11 months, Sean's status had not changed. Heather was now a single parent and did not know whether her baby's father was dead or alive. Not yet Sean's wife, the military did not provide her with much feedback from the numerous inquiries she had made. After another 3 months had passed, Heather assumed Sean to be dead. She then turned her attention towards making plans for the future of herself and her fatherless child.

As it turned out, Sean had indeed been missing in action and had become a prisoner of war. After a year and a half of captivity, he and two other POWs had managed to escape. They were eventually picked up by friendly forces and reunited with their respective military companies. Weak, in poor physical health, and somewhat mentally disorientated, Sean was sent to a United States military hospital in Germany. Following 3 months of recuperation and numerous debriefing sessions, Sean received his discharge papers from the military and was being sent home. While in the hospital, he tried several times to reach Heather by phone. However, the home phone had been disconnected. When he called Heather's work number, he kept getting transferred from one recording to another. While in Germany, he had written Heather two letters but had not received a reply. Although his mind was still a bit foggy with respect to how long it had been since he last spoke with Heather, he was happily excited that the two of them would soon be reunited. Along with his two Purple Hearts, he was now on his way home to forever be with the love of his life.

When he landed at the airport, he did not expect Heather to meet him. He had not informed her of his arrival date, as he himself had not been sure of the exact date. After picking up his bags, he stepped out of the terminal to hail a cab. In his uniform and obvious military luggage, he had no problem with immediately getting a cab.

"Good evening sir. Welcome home," the cabbie said as he got out to open the back door and to put Sean's gear into the trunk.

"It's good to be home," Sean said, as he got into the back seat.

Having loaded Sean's bags in the trunk, the cabbie got into the driver's seat and looked in his rearview mirror.

"Where to, Sir?" asked the driver.

"Pine Crest Village, 2223 Spruce Street," Sean replied.

"Tell me," Sean asked, "How are things going around here these days?"

"Same old crap. Just a different toilet," the cabbie said. "Look, I've been back over a year and I'm still driving a cab part-time. But I suppose it could be worst. Some brothers are just sitting around waiting on their government checks. And it's hard as hell to get an appointment at the VA."

After stopping to purchase a dozen roses, the taxi cab arrived at the address. Sean noticed that all the window shades were drawn and that there was a sign in the front yard that read, For Lease. He asked the driver to wait while he went to check out what was going on. He rang the doorbell twice. No answer. He next rapped on the door several times. There was still no answer. Sean dropped the flowers and kicked the door. Confused and somewhat distraught, he returned to the cab.

"Is everything ok, sir?" the cabbie asked.

"I don't know what the hell is going on, man." Sean angrily replied. "Take me back to that Comfort Inn we passed on the way here. Their vacancy sign was on. But stop at that liquor store first."

Paying cash, Sean rented a single for three nights. He figured that this would give him time enough to find out what was going on. Once in the room, Sean, who was tired, confused and in physical and emotional pain, took two painkillers and washed them down with a huge shot of gin. He turned on the radio and found a Blues station. After a couple more shots of gin, he fell asleep fully clothed.

The next morning, Sean got up, unpacked a few things, and took a long shower. He got dressed and took a taxi to the hospital where Heather had worked. He was shocked to find out that she had resigned some time ago and had accepted an administrative position in a hospital in another state. When he tried to find out the name of the city and the hospital, he was informed that such information was confidential and that since he was not Heather's legal spouse, such information could not be released to him. "Go and screw yourself!" shouted Sean as he left the building.

Returning to his hotel room angry and confused, Sean picked up the gin bottle and took a big drink out of the bottle. He then walked two blocks to the Waffle House to have breakfast. During breakfast, he tried his best to figure out what was going on. Where was Heather? Why was the condo up for lease? Why had she not written to let him know what the hell, was going on? These were some of the thoughts that ran through his mind as he tried to enjoy his breakfast.

After breakfast, Sean made his way to the nearest Wells Fargo Bank to find out the balance in the joint checking and savings account he and Heather had established. Once again he encountered a great shock. The savings account had been closed out and there was only $100.00 left in the checking account! Sean was utterly confused. He was sure that there should have been at least $5,000 in the savings accounts and no less than $1500 in the checking account. After fifteen minutes of going back and forth with the bank manager, he gave up and stormed out of the bank in an angry mood.

Back at the hotel, Sean poured out a half glass of gin and took three painkillers. He sat down on the side of the bed and began to sob. He had never been so devastated and confused in his whole life. Not even during the time he was a POW. For a man who had won two Purple Hearts and who had cheated death and escaped captivity during his time in the Middle East, Sean now found himself in a situation in which he felt completely defenseless. He took another swig of gin. Now a bit buzzed, he began to think out loud to himself. Why has God forsaken me? What great sin have I committed? Jesus, in war, it's kill or be killed. Besides, when you go to war, don't you pray to God to be victorious…even if it means killing your enemy? He waited for God to answer. But the wait was in vain. He got up and went to the bathroom to pee. After peeing, Sean came out of the bathroom and flopped himself across the bed and fell asleep.

All throughout the night, Sean wrestled with nightmares of scenes of the war in the Middle East; particularly, scenes of dead women and children. In one of those nightmares, he saw Heather standing on a hill with a small baby in one arm and waving at him with the other. At first, it seemed as if she was waving and saying, "Hello Honey, it's so good to see you." But then, he realized that she was waving and saying, "Goodbye Honey, we'll see you." He also had a dream of his mother on her deathbed. Her last seven words to him were, "Goodbye son, be a good boy now." What strange bed-fellows do devastation, gin, painkillers, sleep, and turmoil make? Sean would wake up the next morning more exhausted than when he fell asleep. His life was never to be the same.

Sitting up, the man dug deep into his matted hair to reach his itching scalp. This was no easy task. His matted hair made the most dread of dreadlocks look like baby Shirley Temple curls. But Polecat was far from being a Rasta. Despite having been well traveled, he had never been to Jamaica and had little fondness for Reggae music. And his few experiences with ganja had always ended in him becoming extremely paranoid. No; his matted hair was the product of years of accumulated oily dirt and grime that not even a metal rake could comb through.

He stood up, stretched, yawned and allowed his bowels to release the morning's gas. He then looked down at the remnants of what once was probably, a type of smart footwear. The top part of the toe areas had separated from the soles leaving his reptilian-like toes peeking out like turtle heads from their shell. His long, blackened overcoat had a sheen that from a distance may have looked like the shine of the best sharkskin cloth. However, its appearance was likewise due to oily muck accumulated over time. From the two buttons left on the coat, you could tell that it was some type of military coat.

Satisfied that all was well with his footwear and clothing, he picked up the crumpled newspaper and the smelly blanket off of his bus stop bench-bed. He balled up the newspaper and threw it in the trash can that was to the left of the bench. He then folded the smelly blanket and stuffed it into his trusty black garbage bag that held all his worldly possessions.

Mumbling something to himself about the day, he walked behind the faded green bench to relieve his nagging bladder of the morning's fill. He stood there peeing for what seemed like an eternity. When he finally finished, he reached into his black garbage bag and took out a plastic bottle of water. He poured a small amount of water into his cupped hand and washed his face. Clamping his jaws shut and widely stretching his parted lips, he drew his index finger back and forth across his teeth. Now let us get some breakfast, he said to no one in particular.

Looking across the street that ran perpendicular to his, he waved and tipped an imaginary hat to his neighbor, Phew, who had taken up residence on the bus stop bench that was located on the corner where the two streets intersected. Phew had earned his nickname due to the odor he always had.

After the morning salutation, the matted head man grabbed his black garbage bag and walked across the street to the location of the Gospel Bird fast food chicken joint. He went around the back and began rummaging through the garbage bin. In the back right-hand corner of the bin, he found the plastic bag containing last night's leftover chicken and fried okra. "Good boy. Good boy", he mumbled as he gulped down the food.

Despite his seemingly deranged state of mind, he had been befriended by the Night Manager of the Gospel Bird establishment. They had an arrangement that as long as he would not stand outside the establishment and harass the customers, and as long as he would not enter the establishment to use the restroom, the Night Manager would always leave him some of the nights' leftovers in the back right hand corner of the garbage bin located behind the building. To maintain an "A" rating, leftovers could not be stored for the next day, they had to be discarded and written off as a loss. This included the little packs of unopened ketchup, salt, and pepper.

Having finished his leftover chicken breakfast, the matted hair man picked up an old dirty Popsicle stick, broke it in half, and used the end of the sharpest half for a toothpick. He then grabbed his stuffed black garbage bag, threw it over his shoulder, and set out on his daily 5 square mile trek through the community. Each morning, except for Wednesdays, he just seemed to wander aimlessly, going nowhere in particular; but always returned to the bus stop bench before midnight

The bright afternoon sun indiscriminately dispensed its heat over the community. The dirty pee smelling matted hair man, with the black garbage bag over his right shoulder, turned the corner and walked south one block to the Solid Rock Fifth Baptist Full Gospel Missionary Church. He had been on the move for the past six hours, wandering here and there through the community. He looked pitifully tired and hungry. But relief was just steps away. Today was Wednesday and every Wednesday, Fifth Baptist provided a cooked lunch for the homeless. He had become a Wednesday regular.

He entered the huge revival tent which served as a makeshift cafeteria. He made his way to an empty folding table and sat down. Many of the grown-ups and children were happily eating and talking together. And then there were those scattered throughout the crowd who were busy eating and talking with themselves and their invisible comrades. He just sat there looking around as if he was in some fancy restaurant waiting for a waiter to come and take his order.

After a few minutes, a young volunteer came over to where the man was seated and sat a huge Styrofoam plate on the table. The plate was loaded with greens cooked with ham hocks; rice; potato salad; stewed chicken; and cornbread. The young lady rushed back to the serving area and returned with a large plastic cup of red punch. As if imitating a hungry dog, the matted hair man sniffed the food and punch and then began eating.

With obvious disgust on her face, the young volunteer again hurried backed to the serving area and began talking with Mother Steptoe, the President of the Women's Missionary Society. It was the Women's Missionary Society that was responsible for the feeding program every Wednesday. Mother Steptoe, now the Missionary Society President, had been involved in the feeding program for the past 6 years.

"Whew, I almost threw up over there. That man is disgusting," the young lady said to Mother Steptoe.

"Over where, baby?"

"Over there," the young lady said, pointing to the matted hair man.

"Oh, that's old Polecat, darling. He's as harmless as a church mouse."

"Yeah, but the odor from his body is about as harmless as a rattlesnake. And do you see the clothes he's wearing and those supposed to be shoes he has wrapped around his crusted feet? Whew…boy…he stinks! I swear, that man smells like two skunks tied together," the young lady said, as she took out her handkerchief to blow her nose.

"I suppose that's how he got the name, 'Polecat'," Mother Steptoe said.

"What do you mean? I don't get it," the young lady said.

"Child, you're a college student, and you don't know what a polecat is? Lawd a' mercy," Mother Steptoe said, wiping sweat from her face with the bottom of her apron. "Child, a polecat is what we old people call a skunk! One of the deacons said that old Polecat's real name was…" Just then a city bus passed by and the young lady didn't hear what Mother Steptoe had said the matted hair man's name was. And she really didn't care.

"Well, you learn something every day," the young lady said. "That's why I keep telling some of my classmates they need to volunteer some time down here; that you learn more down here than you ever will in our Social Work classes."

Around 11:30 PM, the smelly, matted hair man with the black garbage bag over his shoulder, had completed his rounds and had made it back to his bus stop bench residence. He looked across the street and saw Stanky.

"Goodnight, Stanky," Polecat shouted

"Goodnight, Polecat, see you in the morning," Stanky shouted back.

Polecat bent over, opened his black garbage bag and took out the newspaper he had collected during the day. He carefully spread out the newspaper on the bench. He then sat down and leaned over and pulled out his smelly blanket. As he did so, two clinking sounds were made on the sidewalk. He bent over and picked up the two military medals that had made the clinking sound. Each had a stained ragged ribbon attached to it. He neatly wrapped each ribbon around its piece of metal and put them back into the black garbage bag. He then stretched out on the bench and pulled his blanket up to his neck. He leaned his head over, spat, and whispered to himself, "Another day at the office…good boy." He then turned over on his side.

Pillowing his head with his folded arms, he belched, passed gas, and fell into a deep sleep.

The next morning, looking across the street, Stanky could see paramedics loading Polecat into an ambulance. Startled, Stanky screamed out, "Hey, what y'all done did to old Polecat? Hey...!" With its red lights blinking, the ambulance drove off. In the background, Stanky could be seen standing there scratching his head.

# THE LITTLE OLD BLACK MEN OF THE QUARTERS

Like clockwork, Sugar Man rang the doorbell at exactly 8 AM. TeBow reluctantly pulled himself out of the bed and struggled to the door. "Come on in dude, you know where the coffee pot is," he said to Sugar Man. Sugar Man stepped inside and took a surveying look at TeBow. "Boy, look at you. You look like sheep crap on a rocky mountain. What you do last night? You need to go back to bed and try waking up with a new face. Like Suge Avary would say, you sho is ugly." Sugar Man broke into laughter and closed the door.

"Ah, shut up, man. Go on into the kitchen and turn on the coffee pot," TeBow replied. Yawning and rubbing his eyes with his fingers, he continued. "Me'n Pluck went down by The Dew Drop Inn last night. And boy, did we put one on. Catlac had just come back from his uncle's funeral down in Crabcreek. And he brought back some of that fermented Spring Water. We must have gotten drunker than Coouda Brown…whew…man!" The reference to Coouda Brown came from an old African-American folktale. "Go on and get ready," Sugar Man continue, "we needs to get on down to the Coffee Shop and see what the guys be talking 'bout."

Sugar Man, TeBow and the 'guys' had been friends for a number of years. They were as close as a group of men could be and not be blood brothers. Sugar Man was originally from Louisiana. He had once been herald as the best cane cutter in all of the state of Louisiana. That's how he got the nickname, 'Sugar Man'.

Tebow was a Korean War veteran. He had spent 10 years in the Marines. During those years, he had managed to earn his GED and an Associate Degree in Auto Mechanics. He owned the only auto mechanic repair shop in the 'Quarters'. He was very proud and always bragged that he had a 'staff' of 4 employees.

Catlac had a ten-year-old Coupe de Ville that he kept in mint condition. No matter what the weather was, that car always looked like it just came off the assembly line! It had a shiny red color and the interior was snow white.

When Tebow and Sugar Man got to the Coffee Shop, just about everybody else was already there, T-Bone, Rabbit, Tank, Ice Man and Hockrow. Only Pluck was missing. They had already started ordering breakfast. Grits, eggs, beacon, flat jacks, biscuits, pan sausages, and pork chops. And of course, Hank had that big round piece of Vegas ham; that big slice of ham butt with that little bone in the middle. These men formed a rather eclectic brotherhood.

T-Bone was a carpenter. He had T-bone steak for breakfast, lunch, and dinner! T-bone, eggs, and grits; T-bone and French Fries; T-bone, potatoes, and greens! And he was known to suck on the bone long after he had cleaned it of meat! Yet he had no problem with his weight. And he always seemed to have been in the best of health.

Rabbit was a small man about 5 feet 7 inches. He weighed in at about 163 pounds. His wife was about the same height but weighed a little over 195 pounds. They had married one year after graduating high school. When they celebrated their 12th wedding anniversary, they already had 8 kids. He was now retired from the local Lumber Yard.

Tank was a huge man. He weighed around 310 pounds. Yet he was not fat. In fact, he was said to be as solid as a Sherman Tank! He probably would have been a pro football player had it not been for a freak car accident during his junior year in college. He broke both of his legs. It took him over a year to walk again. However, the doctors had said that a football career was out of the question. Once he regained the ability to walk, he had returned to school, earned his degree and became an assistant high school football coach.

Ice Man worked at The People's Market Place. The People's Market Place had been built on the site of what was once the old ice plant. Ice Man had worked at the old ice plant for about 16 years. When the plant closed down and The People's Market was built on the site, Ice Man was hired and put in charge of the frozen food section and the crushed ice bends.

Buchroe had gone into the military right out of high school. After 25 years in the military, he had retired as a Master Sergeant. During his time in the service, he had had the opportunity to travel all over the world. He could engage in simple conversations in Spanish, French, German and Italian!

Though not formerly educated beyond high school and military training, he had amassed a wealth of knowledge during his travels.

Pluck was a retired machinist. He was known to drink wine daily. While many people struggled to drink 8 glasses of water a day, Pluck had no problem drinking a half gallon of wine daily. Yet, he seemed never to get inebriated. As wine is fermented from plucked grapes, he had earned the nickname, 'Pluck'.

"Moun'n gents," Sugar Man said, greeting everyone.

"How Y'all doing," TeBow chimed in, "Pluck not here yet?"

"Haven't seen him since I had to help him upstairs to his room last night," Tank said, as he cut up his ham into big mouth size chunks. "Boy…we must have talked all night."

"Yeah, I know," said TeBow. "I've been there."

"Oh, he'll probably be here later," Buckroe said.

"Hey! Fannie Mae, you going to take these brother's orders?", T-Bone screamed out to the waitress.

"Oh, shut your mouth Negro," Fannie Mae screamed back. "I already got it cooking. They eat tha same old stuff every day. I always know what they want. And if they were to order something else, I swear, I'd know he must be sick. Hell, I've known them all my life." She then pushed open the swinging door and went into the kitchen.

This group of old men was known as the 'Elders of the Quarters'. They were all well in their senior years. Rabbit was the youngest of the bunch. And he was said to be in his late 60s. Hockroe, the oldest, was said to be somewhere between 85 and 87. No one was really sure.

Although a couple of them still had living spouses, they still met for breakfast at the Coffee Shop every Tuesday, Thursday, and Saturday. And this had been going on ever since the Coffee Shop opened several years ago. Before the Coffee Shop, they always met at the Lodge Hall. Today was Thursday.

After about an hour and a half, Pluck strolled into the Coffee Shop. He must have bathed in the Old Spice because you could smell it as soon as the door was pushed opened.

"Alright, alright, alright…tha Pluck is in tha house," he said. "Oh, I see y'all already started without me. That's cool…that's cool." Looking up,

Buckroe said, "Man, a few more minutes and we'd be ordering lunch. Sit your old butt down."

While Pluck pulled back his chair to sit down, Rabbit started singing, "Things…I use tha do…Lawd…I can't do, no moe…" Everyone seated at the table burst into laughter. "Sing it, boy!" Buckroe shouted. "As old as you are, there are a lot of things you can't do no more!" This time, there was an explosive burst of laughter.

"Ok Brethren, now that Pluck's here, we can get down to business," Buckroe said. "Now we got to do what we got to do to get the Quarters back to the way it used to be. Not like now, with these yung'ns walking 'round with their pants like they trying to get the wind to blow the funk off they butts!"

"Sho you right," T-Bone said, "we got to stop those new style slavers from com'n down here and shackling our youths with that white dope…keeping them outta school and fight'n each other instead of fignt'n who they ought'a be fight'n."

"Yeah, we got to take the village back," TeBow said. "I checked everything out with Catlac last night. That bottle of fermented Spring Water was not the only thing he brought back with him."

"It just don't make no sense", Pluck said, "To have Dr. King to give up his life for nothing. We owe it to him to do what should'a been done long time ago."

"I heard that!" Rabbit said. "It's like what the good Doctor always said, if you ain't found anything worth dying for, you ain't got noth'n much worth living for."

"Alright y'all", Buckroe said. "We'll meet down by the Hall at 10:30 tomorrow night. The grapevine says they're going to be coming down to the Quarters 'bout 11 PM. We need to make sure we're ready. This is going to be the last time they're gonna bring that white dope down here."

Yes, for these old men, the Quarters remained that well-knitted community where everybody always looked out for each other. If you were to ask the young Black children of today what they knew about the Quarters, they would probably start talking about the shiny new 25 cents coins representing the 50 US states. Or they would tell you about the time they had in the French

Quarters of New Orleans, during Mardi Gras. It's doubtful that they would be able to relate the term to what was once called the Slave Quarters.

Following Emancipation, America remained a segregated society. The term Quarters, became popular in designating the geographical residential section of a small city where Black people lived. This was usually across the other side of the railroad tracks that separated the Black and White communities. You know, like the Reservation was the term for where the majority of Native Americans lived; usually separated by a small river or small desert area. The term, The Bottoms, was often used as a synonym for the Quarters.

It must be made abundantly clear that the slave quarters and what became popularly simply known as The Quarters, were as different as night is from the day. Rather than being a squalor living area, The Quarters was an exotic, thriving, self-sustaining, self-owned Black community. A segregated community…yes…but one that was totally integrated into its self. What young Blacks today refer to as the hood, is a far cry from the standards of The Quarters; with its sense of dignity, love, and respect for each other. In The Quarters, Black folks looked out for each other. Back in the day, in The Quarters, old Black men were revered and respected, rather than jeered and disrespected. They were the guardians of the extended families of The Quarters. They were the modern day sages and griots of the African-American community.

The following Saturday morning, all of the Elders of the Quarters arrived at the Coffee Shop around the same time. They stood outside chatting a few minutes before going inside. They talked about the weather, the state of the nation, various things going on around the world, and spoke of widows in the Quarters who were in need of help with different types of home repairs. They all agreed that next week they would visit those widows and attend to their needs. They then went inside to have breakfast.

Inside, Fannie Mae had already set up their booth and table. She informed them that their regular orders would soon be ready. After all the old men had taken their seats, Sugar Man asked if anyone had watched or listened to the early morning news. Catlac was the first to reply.

"When I turned on the TV this morning, they were reporting something about a car missing the curve over there on River Road last night. Said the car crashed right through the railing. Lucky for the driver, the damn thing landed right in the shallow water of the river. Funny thing though, they didn't find no driver nor passenger in the car. But they did find two bags of that white stuff in the car. The news also said that the car was from out of state."

"Now ain't that a trip," uttered TeBow.

"Well, let me tell y'all what I heard this morning," Pluck chimed in. "I was listening to the radio and heard them say that there was a big commotion over in front of the Precinct on 5th Street, last night. And when the popo come out, they found two White boys tied up with notes in their mouths and little bags of that white stuff in their pockets. But that's not all...", Pluck continued, "the reporter said that a note in one of the boy's mouth said, 'stay out', and the note in the other boy's mouth said, 'of the quarters! Ain't that something!'", Pluck concluded.

"My, my," Buckroe said, as he stood up with his glass of water in his hand, "tha Lord really works in mysterious ways. Don't He?"

"Sho, yu right. A toast, gentlemen," Tank replied. They all stood up and raised their glasses of water and shouted, "I Toast!" They then sat down.

"Y'all old men ready to eat now?" Fannie Mae cried out. "Make mine two…medium rare," T-bone shouted back. Loud laughter followed.

As the little old men chatted and enjoyed breakfast and each other's company, music could be heard coming over the Coffee Shop's speaker system. It was Muddy Waters playing and singing, "I Got My Mojo Working…"

# A PEDAGOGICAL ODYSSEY

# PROLOGUE

It had been a long hot day. The air conditions in the classrooms had been put to the test—kept shutting off and on. Sagifo opened the door and entered the office he shared with a couple of other teachers. He pulled the chair back from his desk and sat down. He leaned over to his left and opened the small fridge and took out an eight-ounce bottle of Ginger Ale. He unscrewed the cap and took a long cool drink. He sat the bottle down on the desk and released a small satisfying belch. As he sat there, he found himself drifting into deep contemplation:

*Teach. That's what I do. I teach. How ironic. Thirty-Five years ago, when I graduated undergrad school, the one thing I swore was that I would never do, was to teach. No Sir! I was going to be a successful Black entrepreneur and aid in the growth and development of Black community life through philanthropic activities. Indeed the Lord works in mysterious ways. Thirty-five years in the classroom! Thirty-five years engaged in a labor of love for which there has been very little monetary compensation. Yet, this bitter cup has consumed me with such devotion that I have found it impossible to put asunder. Father God, continue to give me divine pedagogical wisdom and knowledge as well as an undying commitment to my chosen mission as a teacher.*

Despite the years of emotional, economic and educational challenges, Sagifo had refused to let himself to be pulled down into the bowels of endless despair and subsequent defeat as a role model, mentor, and scholar-teacher. He knew that in this quest, he had not been alone. He was well aware that there were others like him who had also chosen to remain in educational quarries of the inner-city classroom.

Although many educational and socio-political changes had taken place in inner-city schools, there still remained old negative stigmas as well as new ones that rode in on the so-called winds of educational changes in inner-city schools. Although many schools have been named after famous African Americans and Latino Americans in the Civil Rights Movement, sports, the entertainment industry, the political arena, and the socio-cultural arenas, conditions for learning remain inadequate. Whereas some of the schools were once looked upon as citadels of the community, today they have become a kind of refuge for a few hours of fun and games; and where put-downs and free for all name-calling have become the social norm. In some schools, the "N" word seems to have become a term of endearment freely used by all irrespective of ethnicity. In all too many of today's inner-city schools, social promotion has become the "educational turnstile" for masses of youths destined to become "run a way" models of the orange attire that has become vogue as the new black and brown.

Such was the current situation that Sagifo and his comrades faced each day. Thus he was not taken aback by the disposition of his young colleague, Rashon, who stopped by the office to

share his frustrations as a young black male teacher trying to make a difference. Entering the office and without speaking, Rashon began pouring out his heart to Sagifo.

"Man, I've tried! But I just don't know if I can do it anymore!"

"What's up, bro?" Sagifo replied.

"I'll tell you what's up. The way people are acting around here, you would think that we're the enemy instead of those screw-ups downtown. Nobody 'round here appreciates what we're trying to do here in this school!" Flopping down on the small couch in the office, Rashon continued. "And another thing…it's hard as hell to try to take care of a family on a teacher's salary! And the nerve of these kids…saying we're just here because it's a job and we don't care whether they learn or not!"

"I hear you brother", Sagifo interrupted. He took another drink of Ginger Ale and continued. "But we need to discern where these young brothers and sisters are coming from. We need to…to…to look at where they are coming from with respect to their mindset. The mindsets that are the result of the mind games played on the kids by the folk downtown and by some of our very own teachers…right here—some of them who are people of color! You know. Those who always referring to themselves as 'Teachers of the Hood'…" Before Sagifo could continue, Rashon cut in.

"That's another thing I'm talking about. As soon as school is out, many of our so-called colleagues…including some who are Black…hop in their cars…find a nice little Happy Hour joint…somewhere between the hood and their little Ricky and Lucy neighborhood…and spend hours sharing how they survived another day of hazard pay duties—working with hopeless little Black and Brown kids who only come to school to get free breakfast and lunch."

Rashon paused for a moment to get a Ginger Ale from the small fridge. Sagifo took advantage of the pause to continue what he had to say. "Believe me brother Rashon", he said, "I know how hard it is for a man…any man…or woman…to try to take care of a family on what they pay us. I know. I got two kids in college…and their mommy to take care of! And while scholarships help out a little, they don't keep school bills and other bills from coming." Sagifo cleared his throat and continued. "Listen, man those freaking colleagues of ours got a higher power to deal with. So don't worry about them."

Looking at Rashon, Sagifo could see that although he was listening, his facial expressions and other physical dispositions gave off vibes of someone who was angry and grappling with disappointment and seeming defeat. Sagifo felt that he was looking at someone who was in dire need of understanding, support, encouragement, and motivation. It was as if he was looking into a mirror of time—seeing a reflection of himself many years ago. He felt that it was not merely by coincident that their paths had crossed. He was more and more convinced that God does indeed work in mysterious ways.

> *Shall I always be a transient soul*
> *Traveling on the stale path of time?*
> *Will turbulent tides of the lived lives*
> *Ever end their to and fro search?*
> *Like Job, God demands that I too,*
> *Be put to the test—I too, must*
> *And will succeed…as we dig our destinies*
> *That the soil of time will bear.*
> *Yes…the harvest remains forever plentiful;*
> *And the reapers still remain but a few.*

"So you understand where I'm coming from", Rashon said. "Before I help someone else, I first got to be able to take care of me and my own. And I understand where you're coming from too, bro. I guess I just need to evolve a new perspective that will enable me to do both. You know…taking care of me and mine and also remaining mindful of the ways and means by which I can help others in the extended family. Lots of work, man…lots of work."

"You know what Rashon?" Sagifo said. "I think you're on to something there."

"What do you mean?" Rashon asked.

"Perspective, brother, a new perspective", replied Sagifo. "If we're going to initiate greater change, then we need to begin with a change in perspective. All of us!"

Rashon eyes grew bright and wrinkles formed in his brow. "You mean like…instead of just looking at things from a revolutionary point of view…maybe we need to focus on looking at things from an evolutionary point of view."

Both men were now excited and well energized. "Yeah, something like that", Sagifo said as he cleared his throat again. "Revolutions come and go…come and go. You know, the more things change, the more they stay the same. But in evolution…check it out…the more things change…the different the environment becomes! Hell man!" Sagifo shouted, "Change is evolutionary!"

"That's deep man." Rashon said. "But I feel you bro. I feel you." He stood up, stretched and began walking around the room as he continued talking. "Look, brother, we've heard all the deliberation on how academically challenge our students are and have been given umpteen rationales for the challenges by those fake educational psychologist who have pawned themselves off as experts on the psycho-neurological learning disabilities of children of color! And the sad thing is that so many of us have bought into this load of crap!"

Rashon had now become well collected and electrified as he continued walking around the room—pounding his left fist into the palm of his right hand. He stopped, turned towards Sagifo and continued. "Look, don't get me wrong", he cautioned. "I'm not saying that we don't have kids that are academically challenged…hell…every ethnic group does! And I'm not making excuses for those kids of ours that just sit on their butts and just don't try—

having been brainwashed that they have an innate inferiority! But you must admit that there is a significant number of our kids that are academically challenged because they have been short change and ignored at the basic levels; and have simply been socially promoted from one grade to another without having mastered the basic problem solving skills for each grade!"

The seriousness and compassion in Rashon's voice had become quite evident. A tear slowly traveled down Sagifo's right cheek. But it and those swelling up in Sagifo's eyes were not tears of sadness; rather they were tears that love, revealed truths, and motivation produces. He had become deeply moved by what Rashon was saying.

"Look Sagifo", Rashon continued, "While we need to take care not to reinforce negative stereotypes, we likewise need to take care not to lower our expectations of our kids…and see them as young, gifted, God created creatures that are worthy of the highest of academic achievement. And speaking of new perspectives, we Black male teachers and mentors must now become academic window washers engaged in washing and wiping away the distorted images our kids have been mirroring. You feel me, Bro? You feel me?"

"I agree my brother", Sagifo replied. "In our new perspective, we need to realize that in each and every child God has sent our way, we need to realize and see that there is a genius locked within them and we must become the key masters to unlock the door releasing that genius within…a genius just waiting to be released." Around this point, the conversation ballooned.

Even the most profound problem-solving conversations have their time frames. The daytime hours were waning and Rashon had to pick up his children from their school's After Care program. And Sagifo had some domestic chores he needed to get done. The two men agreed to continue the conversation later. However, Sagifo had one more thing he wanted to share before they parted.

"Before you go Rashon, let me share a couple of things to think about that an old man once shared with me when I was a young confused college student. I had done something stupid and almost lost my scholarship." Sagifo paused for a moment and then continued. "The old man said to me, Son, I'm just a third-grade scholar. I had to quit school to help out on the farm. But let me say this to you…maybe it'll help…I don't know… Anyway, he went on to say this to me, Think about this, my boy. Before a ship can sail off on its journey, it must be moored and stocked with the necessary things it needs to complete and return from its journey. And before a tree can bear fruits with seeds for a new life, that there tree has to be anchored and nourished by its own roots. And ain't no two ways about it, if you don't have no common sense, you just like a goldfish jumping out of the fishbowl on to the table to be free. "Man, I've never forgotten those words. Yes sir, we got to be dispensers of knowledge, anchored role models and mentors; as well as those who must nourish young minds with wisdom." Emotionally full, Sagifo let out a long sigh, turned to Rashon and said, "Come on man, let's get out of here."

In the parking lot, the two men share a brotherly bear hug, gave each other a fist bump, and headed off to take care of their respective personal duties.

*Arise…you children of now.*
*Wipe away the matter from your eyes;*
*Unplug your waxed ears and hear*
*The whispering echoes of the ancestors*
*Awakening sleepy memories—yawning*
*Visions of deferred dreams reflecting*
*Realities soaring on the winds of change;*
*Come and create new dreams…dreaming back*
*Visions of new realities to come;*

*While holstering fear and releasing fury,*
*Forget not: one is not the masses;*
*While holstering fear and releasing fury,*
*Forget not: the bank of justice practices foreclosure;*
*While holstering fear and releasing fury,*
*Forget not: yours is a generation with a blood debt;*

*My children…let not the orchards of your minds*
*Be victims of mental frostbite*
*Or of the scorching dryness of mental drought;*
*Let not your being linger behind like plucked fruit to rot;*
*Let not time steal away the germinating forces of your seeds;*
*Let not the scythe of time sever your anchored nourishing roots.*
*My children…in the turbulent waters of change,*
*Let not the harsh waves of time wash away the harvest.*

# INTERLUDE

From the late 1950s, to well into the earlier years of the Millennium, Sagifo had seen and experienced a great deal in the social, political, economic, and cultural mobility of Black America. Attempts to bring about desegregation had been usurped by integration. Civil rights, voter rights, and equal employment had become law. He had even lived to see America elect a Black President—twice! Yes, Blacks had come a long way along the journey towards full American citizenship. Yet, at the present time, the masses of Blacks in America are still struggling.

When put into proper perspective, it is realized that it has been nearly some 400 years since that first Dutch frigate landed in Jamestown, Virginia, with its cargo of 20 Black slaves who would be instrumental in laying the foundation upon which would evolve that Peculiar Institution that would give rise to the new Promised Land that would eventually become America: the land of the free and the home of the brave. Indeed, it has been almost 240 years since the signing of the Declaration of Independence—echoing that *all men* were created equal and were entitled to certain unalienable rights: Life, liberty, and the pursuit of happiness. And although President Lincoln signed the Emancipation Proclamation over 151 years ago, Blacks in American are still struggling to achieve full justice and equality in this, their home too. Yes, there remain new challenges to be overcome. And these new challenges require new perspectives and strategies to conquer them.

Saturday evening, Rashon stopped by Sagifo's house for a backyard happy hour. When he arrived, he found Sagifo out back basing barbecue and listening to Joe Henderson's *A Flower Is a Lonesome Thing*. Sagifo, who had dubbed himself to be the ultimate Grill Master, had three different grills smoking at the same time. On one he had baby back ribs. On another was a huge brisket. The third grill was loaded with prime pieces of lamb and goat.

"Sagifo! You got it going on back here. Damn man! It smells good!"

"It's gonna taste even better. Grab yourself a cold one."

"Thanks. Man, I got some heavy thoughts to share with you. Last night I was thinking about what we were discussing yesterday in the office, and it suddenly came to me, the way some of our young students are confused in the way they are thinking. You see, it seems that they feel that their lives are defined by what happens to them. Man, they are failing to realize that their lives are not defined by what happens to them, but rather, by how they respond to those happenings!"

"I hear you my brother", Sagifo said as he tended to the meats on the grills, "and I see where you are coming from. Our kids are hung up on responding to how they are valued in so many negative ways…rather than acting from the perspective of just how valuable they are. Hell, the forces of injustice could care less about us marching and shouting 'No justice! No peace'! That's what the perpetrators of injustice are all about! Giving us no justice and no peace…!"

Sagifo had long held on to the belief that childhood mental, social, cultural and academic growth and development is as much of a metamorphic process as it is for a butterfly before it can wiggle itself out of the womb of its cocoon, flex and fly away on its fragile wings. Oh, but once those wings establish their innate stability, they enable the butterfly to soar triumphantly through the most tempestuous winds.

Sagifo and Rashon were soon joined by a couple of Sagifo's neighbors and two other friends he and Rashon knew. This gathering spent several hours enjoying barbecue, drinks, and deep conversation on how to raise the minds of today's youth that they might evolve new perspectives that would enable them to develop new strategies to meet the new challenges they faced. As the evening hours slowly segued into the early morning hours, the gathering concluded that their responsibility as mentors was to sow germinating seeds in the fertile minds and souls of their young charges and cultivating them with undying love and audacious determination.

*Let us be as crucible steel*
*Forged by the life-fires of ancestors;*
*Let us scratch the itching brains*
*Of the children we have borne.*
*Let us echo the thunder…reflecting*
*The lightening of our triumphs;*
*Let us strengthened new spines of life*
*With the spasms of old victories.*

*Let ignorance disintegrate*
*Like the froth of worn receding waves;*
*Let the dawn of a new day*
*Shatter the darkness of oblivion;*
*Let our tenacious determination*
*Leave footprints in the mud of hope;*
*Let our children rise above the levees of inhibition.*

The backyard new perspective forum ended around 3 A.M. After all his guest had departed, Sagifo shuffled inside the living room and flopped on the couch. Despite the sandman weighing sleep upon his weary body, a plethora of thoughts on the evening's and early morning's conversation flowed through his mind. These eventually lead to focus on the parable of the seed: But there were some that fell on rich soil, and produced fruits…and grew. Fueled and energized by the profundity of this parable, Sagifo arose from the couch and slowly walked to his study and sat down at his computer. As tired as he was, he felt it necessary to write down what he was now thinking—least he should forget or his old ally, time, would intervene in his life before he could verbally share these thoughts:

Beloveth children—buds of hope—flowers of promise—as you continue to blossom along life's awesome sojourn through these times of trials and tribulations, realize that you do not journey alone. In times of doubt, remember that The Great Benign Power of the Universe is journeying with you. So are we—your elders—and all the ancestors. Continue to strive to discover the flow of your destinies—realizing that the choices you make along the way, will determine whether or not you reach determined destinations. Never forget that each and every one of you is endowed with special gifts that make you valuable to the human race as a whole.

As the minutes slowly ticked into the next hour, Sagifo, struggling to muscle the weight of his eyelids, continued. *As you continue to journey, learn to accept each crisis as an opportunity to overcome adversity. To do this, know that the Supreme Architect of the Universe has given each of you different sets and arrangements of talents and abilities in various degrees; and these will enable you to turn dreams into visions…and visions into realities. Indeed you are those we have been waiting for…*

No longer able to press the weight of his eyelids, Sagifo move the computer mouse to Save As, and typed, PEDAGOGICAL ODYSSEY. He then clicked, Save. Satisfied, he turned off the computer. With the last bit of strength he had left, Sagifo, pushing down on the floor with his feet, while at the same time pushing down of the arms of the chair with his hands, slowly rose and literally drag himself back to the couch. The last thoughts echoing from the silent womb of his mind before falling into a deep sleep were…*the work goes on…only the worker dies…the work goes on.*

# EPILOGUE

Indeed, the work goes on. In blistering irony…it goes on. Despite so many have lived to see a great deal of the 'Dream of Black America' come into vision…despite so many Black Americans have made it to the mountaintop…and even some may have gone on down the other side into the valley of the new Promised Land, there are still left on the downside of the mountain, a confused meandering generation that is reminiscent of Sisyphus. Yes, only the worker dies…the work goes on:

*The day stops. Night begins.*
*The cocooned dream hangs lazily*
*On the leaf of time;*
*The veiled goddess—justice*
*Remains oblivious; her skewed scales*
*Mimic a fake balance.*

*The dream…dreams back to us*
*A Mona Lisa smile…*
*Teasing the realities of our beings…*
*Zip lining through winds of change…*
*Sailing over cobwebbed roads*
*We once marched down…*

Printed in the USA
CPSIA information can be obtained
at www.ICGtesting.com
LVHW062303200823
755603LV00016B/892